# Color Me Successful

## HOW COLOR SELLS YOUR BRAND

### Book 1 - Color Theory

### What Each Color Means for Your Small Business

by Judy Haar

Copyright 2017 by Judy Haar. All Rights Reserved.

No part of this publication may be reproduced, distributed or transmitted in any form or by any means without the expressed permission of the author except in the case of very brief quotations. The author has tried to express her opinions from her knowledge base and every effort has been made to accurately represent the content but there is no guarantee as to the accuracy of any interpretations of this information. Nothing in this Book or the Series of Books is a promise of success or guarantee of earnings based upon the reader's choices, only suggestions. You alone are responsible for your actions, choices and results for your business. It should be clear that the author makes no guarantees that you will achieve any results from her ideas or models presented in this Book or Series or on her site. No liability can be assumed regarding how the information is applied to your particular personal situation. There is clearly no guarantee on the results achieved from using this information.

Get more information at
http://www.emergencepublishinggroup.com/
Other Books by Judy Haar
For I Am With You
Death Tones: Short Stories About Transformation
Color Me Successful: How Color Sells Your Brand: Book 1 Color Theory
Color Me Successful: How Color Sells Your Brand: Book 3 Color Marketing
Follow the Light - Write Your Journey

**Books in Color Me Successful Series to Come**
Color Me Successful: How Color Sells Your Brand: Book 4 Color Help
Color Me Successful Workbook. Building Your Brand and Marketing
**Book in Emergence Series to come**
Re-Emergence

# Table of Contents

## Why I Wrote This Book and Why You Should Read It

## Introduction

### Chapter 1:
The Beginning

### Chapter 2:
Just The Stats

### Chapter 3:
Why Is Color Important

### Chapter 4:
Why Do We See Color

### Chapter 5:
Color Theory and The Beginning of Everything You Need to Know

### Chapter 6:
Color Harmony

### Chapter 7:
The Color Wheel and How Color is Used

### Chapter 8:
Conclusion

## Appendix
References

**Extra Section: Color Blindness**

**Assignment**

**About the Author**

## **Why I Wrote This Book**

This Series, four in all, is for small business owners and future owners. Even if an artist or painter, if your next idea is selling your work, you must understand color. Are you a designer? Your business is about the use of color. Do you paint rooms and homes for a living, color is key. Yes, color is important to most, but this Series can not cover all aspects of its use. What this Series is about is the use of color for small business when branding, marketing, merchandising, developing a website and sales.

I have worked with small business for the past twenty years, and one thing I have noticed is how many have terrible brands with little forethought into how important this one thing is. The brand is off, the color all wrong and the logo drives business away from the owner. When I searched for help on this issue, little was published. Not until I was part of a company who did successful branding did I learn that the first and most important thing to do for your business is to develop a successful brand, a brand that can grow and drive business to your door. From your brand, the small business owner can then create a website and strong marketing material. I suspect that you, the small business owner, cannot afford to spend millions, but you still need a brand that is remembered and sells while your website and marketing material give tremendous growth opportunity and support.

Why did I write this Series? Not much accurate information exists on how to develop a great brand and marketing material for your business. We know that buying is about emotion, and what in your brand and marketing material delivers the emotional punch, color. The first thing your customer sees and remembers is color. Did you know that color can affect a blind person as well? I talk about this at the end. Color is energy waves and affects all living things, so how important is color, the most. This book is all about its use to drive business to your door, to help you understand how color does this and what colors you should use. Until now, this process was not clearly defined; I am pleased to bring the theory to the small business owner. You need to be successful, thrive and use everything at your disposal to succeed so welcome to the first in the Series, 'Color Me Successful, How Color Sells Your Brand: Book 1 - Color Theory.'

## **Why You Should Read This Series**

The biggest mistake that small business makes is not creating a brand and strong sales materials that their customers will remember and buy. It is important that you do this one-step RIGHT the first time because once it is done, it is hard to change. If you have a great brand then it becomes essential that you, the small business owner, understand how color affects your messages through your website and marketing material. You must first have a cursory understanding of color theory and how all this evolved. Book 1 in the Series plans to do just that.

Did you know that your brand could drive business away from you, as well as to you? Did you know that shopping is emotionally based and did you know that color was the most important thing in your brand, and marketing material to control emotion? You have 90 seconds, probably less, to make your mark, don't waste it with inferior material. After counseling 100's of small businesses, I found most don't understand the first thing about color and how to use it effectively. That is why I wrote this book and you should read the Series, to give <u>the small business owner</u> the knowledge to use color and create the best brand, website and marketing material, ever. Yes, you can do it!

This first, Color Theory, is all about color, its history, and understanding, how we see color and how the color wheel works. This presents basic color theory but enough for the small business owner to be successful. Future Books in the Series will discuss cultural impacts, branding, marketing material creation, color in electronics such as computers and finally, a detailed discussion of each primary, secondary and tertiary color, plus so much more.

By delving into the basics, you will uncover the truths, disregard the rumors, and pick the colors that best describe your business and you, while you influence future sales, emotional ties and physiological reactions. You will learn that color affects us all.

# **Introduction**

What colors should you use in your brand, your website, marketing and material to communicate? One of the most important questions you, a small business owner, need answered. Color can drive customers to your business or turn them away. Over 90% of the visuals that people remember about your brand and marketing material relates to color. Do you own a fast-food restaurant; consider the color **YELLOW** in your brand. Are you a retailer selling high-end clothes, consider a background of **BLACK** and add a splash of elegance in **GOLD** or **SILVER**. Perhaps you are a nonprofit helping stop drug addiction; **WHITE** combined with **BLUE** might be your best bet. Does your brand scream excitement and action, consider **RED**. Look around you, color is everywhere. You are warmed, excited, depressed and even angered by it. Drive by a garden in bloom and marvel at its beauty or be depressed by the black clouds bringing in a coming storm. Color affects our lives in many ways and is a powerful tool for communication. Color can drive immediate, automatic reactions or learned control from cultural differences and experiences. Learn, get on board, this is the most important decision you will make for your small business recognition.

No two people see color the same, our eyes are all different. Many cultures create different meanings for colors, which can also influence a response. Combinations of different colors together can change meanings, as well. This can be a complicated subject. Every person relates to it from personal experience and learned reaction. The science of color is not complete or completely understood, but there are some basic generalities that may help you utilize it to enhance your quest. The first rule of applying color to your business should be honor your taste and trust in your choices, but a little help, hopefully from this Series can give you the right ideas. The science of how it affects human behavior is a branch of behavioral psychology, what actions we may take when viewing color. Many debate over hunches and misconceptions with little research supporting either. By understanding the reasons for color reaction, you can successfully use it to enhance your brands, logos, advertising and marketing. Color will help drive people to your business, product or service by re-enforcing feelings and make them buy from you. It is critical in product design and signage. Color has the power to alter the way our brain relates to the outside world. How can color do this? You will learn in a future chapter.

We will be looking at some conflicting information and discussing where the conflict might arise. Book 1 Color Theory will lay out a solid foundation for its use on your business. Remember, although this Series will try to give the majority of explanations and options, color psychology is new, and the choices are up to the reader, you. I can only relate what experience exists. Finally, this will show you how to apply what you learn, so let us start at the beginning..

Depending on the customer base and hues, tints, shades, cultural differences, context, emotion, plus all manner of other things, the actual colors you choose need tested against your market. We will be suggesting where a color might be used successfully and looking at some examples. Let's get started on our exciting journey, picking the right colors for your small business.

# **Chapter 1 The Beginning**

From the very beginning of the human race there was the sun, the sky, and water, we have always had color. Although, the interpretation of color differed over time, the rays from the sun have always existed for hope to the human race. The sun is where the history of color started, after all, color is light and energy and light comes from the sun.

There is evidence that thousands of years ago, people attempted to use color in healing and therapy, called chromo therapy. Different cultures, from the advent of society, interpreted color in various ways and with different names. It is indeed an interesting subject that has been around from the beginning of time.

We pick up the story in 1613 when d'Aguilon authored a book discussing not only the optics of the eye but the behavior of light and color. Produced for the use of painters and artists, he supported the theory of primary colors. Remember, colors were created from the pigments that existed at that time, so a primary color was a pigment color.

Picture 1 Prism

Our recent understanding started in 1665 with a man called Isaac Newton. He was attending Trinity College in Cambridge when the plague broke out, and Trinity was closed for two years. He was 23 years old at the time and not recognized as being scholarly, but history will tell of his genius. Discussed here, relating to color, he discovered 'The Theory of Optics.' At that time, prisms were used, but it was widely believed that when the sunlight was passed through a prism it was the impurities in the prism that caused the color rainbow on the wall to emerge. Isaac ran an experiment. He closed his shutters for darkness and made a single hole for the sunlight, one small pure ray of sunshine emerged. Isaac passed this through a prism, which produced a spectrum of colors. Using a second prism, he recomposed the multicolored spectrum into white light proving that impurities in the crystal did not cause the colors. Newton also showed through this experiment that color, whether scattered or reconstituted stayed the same. His biggest discovery regarding color was; it existed through varying wavelengths and energies, and was not produced by impurities in objects. He could combine certain wavelengths to form other colors such as red light mixed with yellow to produce orange. Others canceled each other out such as yellow and purple to produce white light. Each spectral color represented by its individual wavelength or frequency was unique. Newton's explanation of color was not in material substances but the refraction of light as it spread apart by a prism. In 1942 a man named Goldstein proposed a guide on the effects of color, red/orange stimulating, and green/blue, quieting and agreeable. Other experiments interpreted Goldstein's proposal regarding wavelengths: longer wavelength, such as red, are arousing while shorter wavelengths of colors in the visible spectrum are calming. Each spectral color is represented by its own wavelength or frequency.

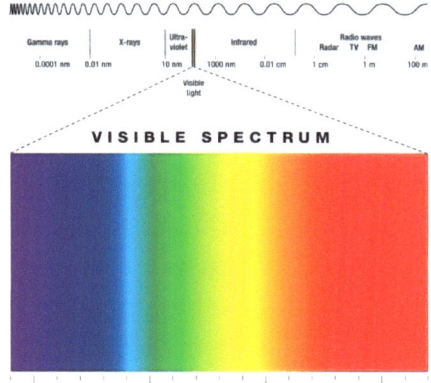

Picture 2 Spectrum

Original color theory in the print world formulated three primary colors: red, yellow and blue (RYB) because these colors were believed to lead to all others and could not be created from any. Long used by printers, and painters, they became the foundation of 18th-century color usage and still, 400 years later are used. Remember, pigments for printing and art were needed.

Picture 3 CMYK Color Model

Invented in 1934 by Murray, the cyan, magenta, yellow and black model (CMYK) evolved to become effective in inks and dyes for photos and a new primary color model was adopted.

Picture 4 RGB Color Model

The primary colors on a computer screen are red, green and blue (RGB) based upon Newton's spectrum of wavelengths. After all, the human eye experiences color.

The rods and cones of the retina come in red, green and blue detecting varieties, but more on that later. However, the rules of behavior for paint, ink or pigment are different from the rules of color in the form of energy.

I have just barely touched upon the theory's explained more completely in Chapters 5, 6 and 7. The purpose is to try to understand the reaction that your customers have to your brand, website, advertising and marketing for your small business. For this, basic color theory understanding is critical.

## Chapter 2 Just the Stats

I came across these statistics while doing research. Can't claim how accurate but an interesting read. Most are probably intuitive, and many have been repeated several times. Analyzing the reactions to color is relatively new, so are most of the stats, but some are ancient. It is interesting to decide just what might be true and what you would have guessed as inaccurate.

*Statistics*

- Women don't like gray, orange, and brown. They like blue, purple, and green
- Research has reinforced that 60% of the time people will decide if they are attracted or not to a message - based on color alone!
- In a survey on color and gender, 35% of women said blue was their favorite color, followed by purple (23%) and green (14%).
- 33% of women confessed that orange was their least favorite color, followed by brown (33%) and gray (17%).
- Just a small percentage of women choose pink as their favorite color.
- Men don't like purple, orange, and brown. Men like blue, green, and black.
- Colors are responsible for 62-90% of our first impressions of brands.
- 80% of visual information is related to color.
- 85% of shoppers place color as a primary reason for why they buy a particular product.
- 40% of the people worldwide would choose blue as their favorite color.
- Some studies show that women prefer warm colors while men, cool colors.

- Color is unique in the sense that it can attract specific types of shoppers and change shopping behavior.
- Carl Jung encouraged his patients to use color in their paintings to express the deepest unconscious part of their psyches.
- Healing through the use of color goes back 2000 years.
- A white box psychologically weighs actual, while a yellow is seen as weighing 10% more than actual and a black box 80% more than actual.
- Color can affect appetites. Yellow can increase your appetite while purple can decrease it.
- Color affects the feeling of time. Red will drive people from a room significantly faster than blue.
- A visual appearance can be more effective then the name.
- For most people, the first decision of the day is color harmony, picking clothes to wear.
- Chromophobia (also known as Chromatophobia) is the rare, persistent, irrational fear of colors.
- Red can mean love and anger, a contradiction, so context is extremely important.
- Red can physically increase heart rates, respiration, and metabolism.
- Purple reflects the planet Jupiter.
- Purple was the first dye ever made by man. It was called Mauveine and was made out of coal tar.
- More shades of white are available commercially than any other color.
- In church, the meaning of a white garment is a sinless life.
- A black cat crossing your path is considered bad luck in many cultures.
- The white belt in Judo represents innocence, purity, and virginity of the soul and mind.
- In the financial arena, red symbolizes a negative direction.

- Bees can't see red, flowers that are red are pollinated by birds, butterflies and wind.
- 75% of the pencils sold in the United States are painted yellow.
- Mosquitoes are attracted to the color blue twice as much as to any other color.
- Owls are the only birds that can see the color blue.
- Powder blue is often used in products to promote cleanliness and purity.
- Blue is the favored color choice for toothbrushes.
- The color green signifies mystical or magical properties in the stories of King Arthur.
- Road cones and barrels marking areas not accessible are in orange. Wearing an orange vest means safety since it can be seen over long distances.
- 33% of the top brand's logos use the color blue.
  29% of the top brand's logos use the color red.
  28% of the top brand's logos use black or grayscale colors.
  13% of the top brand's logos use yellow or gold colors.
  05% of the top brand's logos use more than two colors.
  95% of the top brand's logos use one or two colors.
- 41% of the logos use text only (stylized type).
  09% of the logos don't feature the company name at all.
  93% of the logos are simple enough to be viewable in smaller sizes.
  03% of the logos feature people in their designs.
  13% of the logos use the brand's initials in their design.
- Studies have shown that a product's color influences 60 to 80 percent of a customer's purchasing decision, meaning color can make or break a product.

- Almost 90% of people's assessment on goods or services is based on colors alone.
- Due to colors' strong influence on moods and feelings, their association with products can influence our attitudes and affect purchasing power towards brands.

Interesting statistics don't you think? There are many more where these came from and if you are interested, check the back the appendix, for references.

# **Chapter 3 Why Is Color Important**

Why is color important seems like a simple question but it is quite complex. Every visual stimulus processed by the human brain contains color information. The lack of scientific experimentation makes accurate conclusions on reaction to colors at best, guesswork. More is coming in research, but association with color and reaction to observing the response still provides no answer as to why. Also, color is viewed through relationships, for example, black is perceived as evil and death. Therefore, it is associated with aggressive behavior. This is not a very scientific analysis to support the study of color. In this Series, we will discuss the elementary meanings and help guide the reader to an understanding of how it is used effectively for your business brand, but first we need the basics. Just what is color?

Let us make it simple. Color is energy, each color on a different frequency, vibration or wavelength. Objects absorb certain wavelengths and reflect others back to our eyes. The age old question, is an apple red, through this definition, is no. It just absorbs all light but reflects to our eyes only red. Our eyes pick up the color through cone receptors further defined in Chapter 4. A signal is sent to our brain to interpret what we see. How color is defined lies outside our brain and body but the meaning and reaction lies within our brain. How our brain interprets the color we see is the driving force to understanding how to use it.

That is not the end to discovering how to use color but only the beginning. Please consider that each color is open to numerous interpretations, based on experiences. In other words, colors mean different things to different people in different contexts. It is felt and learned through emotion, cultural, physical reaction and behavior. While some universal meanings exist for colors, it is important to understand a little deeper into differences and how it is used. For example, if you have a business that is a deep-sea fishing experience, blue, even dark blue signifying the ocean, might fit into your scheme. However, if the company specializes in BBQ ribs, a dark blue color, which can be associated with rotten food, might not be good for business. Red, another color with many meanings, needs to be examined closely. For example, red can wake people up and produce excitement, so, if your business is selling a red convertible roadster, this is good. However, another meaning for red can be fear. A horror movie might adopt a red background for advertising. Remember, the devil is simulated as fire, red and evil. Red was also used in the Soviet Union for Communism, so if you are exporting your product to Russia you may want a different color. It is not an accident that adult websites use lots of reds and blacks for the sexual connotation. Ever search for a toy site? You will see plenty of bright colors, ones that are popular with children. Color interpretations vary with age, gender, culture and mood. Confused, overwhelmed? Do not be, the beginning is meant to give you a background when choosing a color for your business brand, yourself and your marketing.

Do not be fooled by the standard lists presented for each color in Chapter 2, as 'generic color definitions'. These are commonly used descriptors, not scientifically based.

Another example; blue, black and purple can be associated with rotting meat. Blue is the most popular 'favorite' color and can mean security, truth, and stability. Purple is interpreted as spiritual, intelligence and perhaps wealth. It can instill emotions of royalty. Black is bold and strong. Some associate it with elegance while others associate black with depression. It is all about where these colors are used and what emotions relate to them through culture, education, instinct, and application. Context, how and where a color is used, is an important word in color psychology.

An experiment to test the brain and physical connection involved four glass bowls, each a different color. They were filled with red, yellow, green and blue jello that was odorless and tasteless. A group of people were brought in, all blindfolded, and tasted each bowl. No odor or taste was reported. Un-blindfolded, the group of people, tasted each bowl, again. The red tasted like strawberries, yellow like lemons, green like a tart apple while blue was the least tasty. The brain experienced and interpreted the colors under different circumstances.

One thing is for sure; color is here to stay and is an evolving process in understanding reactions. You must spend time and effort on the analysis with regards to an emotional response produced from your client to inspire him or her to buy or use your product/s.

Let me recap, reactions to color are emotional, cultural, taught, instinctual, and sometimes physical. The context of how and where the color is used can create a reaction, as well. As we move through this Series, I will use examples to talk about it and how it applies to your business brand, what product you sell or service you provide. At the end of this Series, you will be able to answer all of your questions and more. Exciting? You betcha.

Color Theory will start out defining warm versus cool colors, the color wheel, background color use, tones, shades, tints and mixing and finally, basics for print, art, and electronics. I will tell you where to start, and how-to pick your colors.

## **Chapter 4 How Do We See Color**

Do you care how color is processed? Well, maybe not, and for that reason, this is not a detailed look on this subject. We will delve into the subject a little, just to see a hint of how and why we may, at times, respond to certain colors. Yes, we are talking about brand, advertising, selling and driving the public to your doorstep through color, so, bear with me on this, the chapter is short, and I think you need to know a little more than you do.

Color is a visible spectrum of light, different wavelengths or energies as shown in Chapter 1. As the specific wavelengths hit an object, the surface of that object absorbs light and then reflects the light wavelength, color that is not absorbed. Your eyes take in this reflected color through your pupil, which goes to your lens, and reaches cone and rod receptors in the back of your retina. Rods show us the world in black and white, in dim setting and at dusk. Cones, in bright light, are sensitive to three main colors: red, green and blue (RGB model) which are then sent to your brain and produces reactions. Color is a function of interpretation <u>by your brain</u>. Let me repeat this critical statement, color is a function of interpretation by your brain, in fact, your hypothalamus. A series of signals are sent from this part of your brain to the pituitary gland, then the endocrine system and finally the thyroid. Why is this important? The thyroid controls the release of hormones that drive emotion.

All people perceive color differently because we all have different backgrounds relating to culture, education, learned reactions, behavioral, instinctual and emotional balance. Even though this may be true, colors universally instill some common reactions.

By now you may be screaming, what does this have to do with you and your brand? It has a lot to do with you. Color is in the brain and how you perceive it. The brain can influence immediate reaction, such as red causing a rise in blood pressure and blue decreasing blood pressure, the two colors that physically affect the human body. As you go through the colors, keep in mind how your brain reacts instinctually to some of them, and factor this into your choices, particularly cultural. A good example of this might be red, a confusing one at best. Culturally, red in China can mean good luck while red in Russia can refer to Communism. Red can mean the devil and evil in one context while love in another.

   Some people have color blindness. The most common impairment is red and green, dichromatism, that causes these two colors to appear indistinguishable. Colorblindness is very common, about 9% of all humans, men more than women. People with total color blindness are very rare. However, even people with some color blindness feel it, since it is a wavelength of light of a specific energy that can be sensed, although somewhat differently. If your product or service can relate to the colorblind, you must take this into account when picking colors. More discussion on this subject is included in the extra section at the back of this book, Color Theory.

   For thousands of years, color has been used in the cure of illnesses and to promote health. It has long been known that different colors cause different effects. In other words, our skin sees in Technicolor, confirmed by the noted neuropsychologist, Kurt Goldstein, in his modern classic, *The Organism*.

   New frontiers in blindness may introduce thermal color through the tongue. Won't that be interesting when the theory is fully developed?

# Chapter 5  Color Theory and the Beginning of Everything You Need to Know

This is the start to understanding how to use color. I will repeat some important concepts, delve deeper into explanations and bring you up to where you need to be to have a basic understanding of the use of color. From there, you can jump into the waters of creation and the fun part of this Series.

It must be noted here, again, that the color systems used by scientists and artists are entirely different. An artist will mix blue and yellow paint to get green; while a scientist will mix green and red light to create yellow. We are discussing two different creations of color, one that is tangible on the surface of an object, such as a painted picture (subtractive) and another where light waves are combined to produce an image, like on a computer screen (additive). In the subtractive model used in art and printing, all colors added together become black, while in the additive, all colors added together become white light. Newton proved this. Let's learn even more.

Picture 5 RYB primary colors

In the beginning, color theory was in terms of the three primary colors: red, yellow and blue (RYB). This was when pigment, printing and art ruled the scene. Three primary colors begat three secondary and six tertiary colors. These are subtractive colors or in other words, by adding one pigment to another, a new color emerges. A color circle, based on red, yellow and blue, is traditional in the field of art, has been for the past 400 years and is still in use. Sir Isaac Newton developed the first circular diagram of colors in 1666. Used by artists, this color wheel is, in fact, very limited. The old saying, all colors are made by mixing the original colors of red, blue and yellow, which can't be broken down further, is not true. To compensate, scientists and artists have studied and designed numerous variations of this concept. Differences of opinion about the validity of one format over another continue to provoke debate but truthfully, any color wheel could have merit if presented logically.

In today's world, the simplest understanding of color usage is through the original primary color wheel, RYB but there are two others frequently used, RGB, and CMYK. We will delve into these deeper for a better understanding and a reminder of the color wheels for different applications. This is important and bears repeating. What is your business? Do you need to address two color wheels or more? The answer is probably yes.

Picture 6 CMYK primary colors

As time passed, the artists' color theory was adapted to primary colors most effective in inks or photographic dyes: cyan, magenta, and yellow (CMY). In printing, dark colors are created by the addition of black ink, known as the CMYK system. The CMYK system is an economical way of producing a wide range of colors for printing. CMYK is a subtractive color model, which means colors are created through absorption of particular wavelengths of light. The wavelengths of light that do not get absorbed are reflected. The reflected light ends up being the color we see. The age-old question of 'is an apple red' is now answered by this theory. Red is the only color the red apple reflects, all others are absorbed. You may argue that the apple still is not red; it is the color that is being reflected, but come on, let's keep this simple, shall we?

Picture 7 RGB primary colors

What's next? At the start of this chapter, I mentioned another primary color scheme, this one is used for electronic devices such as computers, mobile phones, and television screens. A different set of primary colors emerges; red, green and blue violet (RGB), modeled through the additive mixture of three monochromatic lights. We have already discussed the RYB model used in art. What about computers, screens, and other electronic applications? What do they use? The RYB doesn't have enough options, but the RGB additive scheme does. Red, green and blue dots are creating the image through a system that uses light. When overlap occurs yellow appears.

Remember the previous discussion on the Retina of the eye, and the cones, and rods? It bears restating. Rods show us the world in black and white, in dim setting and at dusk. Cones, in bright light, are sensitive to three main colors of light: red, green and blue (RGB model) which is then sent to your brain and produces a reaction to color. Color is a function of interpretation by your brain. Each person's brain experiences things differently from someone else. You are probably scratching your head and saying to yourself, how do I pick the right colors for my business? All will become reasonably clear through this Series. The purpose of touching upon color theory is to give you, the small business owner, a glimpse into how important color is and how important it is to pick the right ones.

Let me summarize this chapter before we tackle the color wheel. We talked about the primary colors: red, blue, yellow. They were used by artists, still are, and in the past, printing. Although thought to produce all other colors, this was proven inaccurate.

Printing today uses the cyan, magenta and yellow primaries (CMY) with black (K) to provide the needed colors. Both the RYB and CMYK are subtractive; we see the color of the object through absorption and reflection. You can physically touch the colors, now touch the red apple.

Electronics such as a television, computer screen, or cell phones use the RGB, red, green blue, color scheme. Our cones see these three colors and make other colors through addition of wavelengths of light. This is called additive.

Why do you need to know all of this? You need to understand the basics to be able to pick the right colors for your small business. You may use one color scheme for your print (business cards, marketing material) and another for your website and online press. Picking the right colors gets down to three categories that are useful and fundamental: color harmony, the color wheel, and context, how and where the colors are used.

# Chapter 6 Color Harmony and Context

According to the Merriam-Webster dictionary, harmony can be defined as a pleasing combination or arrangement of different things. Harmony is something that creates a balance and order, equilibrium of things. What harmony is not: chaotic, duller, complex. Harmony, in color theory, is the combination of colors that produce a pleasing effect.

This may sound easy, but it is not. Color harmony is affected by how our brains visualize color, feel emotions, cultural differences, taught/learned response, and other things such as age, gender, and race. Context, where and how the colors are used, has a tremendous impact, as well. Add to this, the difference in colors as pigments and wavelengths of light, such as a painting versus a cell phone screen.

According to the work done by the CIE in the 1930's (Commission Internationale de l'Eclairage, human perception of color), it seems we can see 2.4 million colors. Other unrelated studies have a broad range of maximum colors that the human eye can see from 1 million to 10 million colors. Take your choice, but whatever number you choose, this is many colors to consider. Also, because more cones are in the center of the eye, color is typically seen better in the center, and less so in the periphery.

At one end, a bland color will not engage your customer while a chaotic experience will drive your customer away. The goal is to reach a color harmony of equilibrium, a pleasing visual to engage your customer to remember your brand, site, and product, i.e. context.

We will be discussing some suggestions with the color wheel that will help you work through the confusions and come out with the perfect choices, just stay tuned.

Let us start by taking a look, for example, of how color is influenced by other colors and how it behaves in relation to each other.

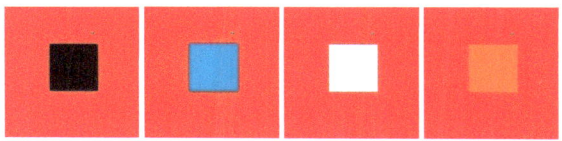Picture 8 color influence by other colors

The orange appears lifeless on a red background while the black on the red background has power and contrast. The white adds purity while surrounded by the red of action giving the viewer the feeling of honesty and trust while driving the client to act. The color of blue says intelligence and calms while the red is clearly energy and action, a conflict. If you add white to this, you have a learned response, American. Perhaps the color of blue-green might produce a better effect for action and harmony. Look below to see. This combination seems to pop more than the above hue of blue does.

Picture 9 color influence

Although examples, this gives you some ideas of color harmony and context. Now let us move to the next principle of color theory, the color wheel.

# Chapter 7 The Color Wheel and How Color is Used

First impressions are everything and there is nothing more important than picking the right colors for your business brand as we have said many times before in this. Let us spend a little time with the color wheel and talk briefly about how to use it.

Picture 10 RYB primary colors

The traditional color wheel, as discussed in a previous chapter, was based upon the primary colors of red, yellow and blue. Many battles have ensued on the validity of this traditional wheel versus others but, in reality, it doesn't matter so long as the wheel presents a logical group of colors. Some wheels may add more colors while others less. For these examples, I will use the primary colors of red, yellow and blue equally spaced around the wheel, to keep it simple.

Picture 11 color wheel

I will then add three secondary colors, green, orange and purple, created from the combining of the primary colors and six tertiary created by mixing a primary with a secondary for a twelve color wheel. All others are formed by mixing the three traditional **primary** colors: red, yellow and blue. If you mix two primary colors, you get

**secondary**: green, orange and violet. **Tertiary** are made by mixing secondary colors with primary colors, so you end up with red-violet, blue-violet, blue-green, yellow-green, red-orange, yellow-orange and so forth. Keep this in mind as we go through mixing, tinting, shading and other definitions. This is the typical artist's wheel.

  Color must function successfully on several different levels, but it is all about your client and what they perceive. Color must first capture the attention of your customer, secondly, it must transfer an action that must be performed, and thirdly, it must be accurate for its particular usage, technology versus print. The colors that you pick must represent the company mission while sustaining and enhancing your clients interest.

  Color combinations are called schemes. Different combinations create a style, and appeal. A basic scheme might use two colors that look good together and send a message that you want your customers to receive. Designs that are more complicated could use a combination of many. Color schemes can also involve shading and tinting for different affects. Brands typically use no more than three colors but usually less. Let's take a look at some of the schemes you may wish to use. We will be discussing Hue's below, so this is a perfect time to define this word.

  *Hue*

<u>Another word for each of the colors on the color wheel.</u>

  Green, orange, yellow is a *hue* of a color. A rainbow shows the melting of one hue into another, from red to violet, and all shades in between. (vocabulary.com)

  The family consists of three primary, three secondary and six tertiary. By adding two different colors together, you can create any number of other colors also defined as a hue. Hues are the purest and brightest colors. Each can be altered by a tint, shade or tone defined below.

Picture 12 Monochromatic

*Monochromatic Scheme*
The use of one color in various shades.

Monochromatic are all the colors (tints, tones, and shades discussed below) of a single hue. The energy is more subtle and peaceful due to a lack of contrast but can also be boring due to a lack of diversity.

Picture 13 Complimentary

*Complementary/Complimentary Scheme*
Colors opposite each other on the color wheel.

If not diluted, they can create maximum contrast and make your image pop. Both colors stand out yet the contrast results in harmony. A cool color across from a warm color looks the best. Look at the color wheel and pick some of your choices, I picked yellow/purple to demonstrate but another might be blue/orange. These colors create a vibrant look and an energetic feel but be careful; they can also overwhelm.

Picture 14 Analogous

*Analogous Scheme*
Colors side-by-side on the color wheel.

Analogous colors are adjacent to each other on the wheel, with one being more dominant, which tends to be a primary or secondary color, and two on either side complementing, which tend to be tertiary. To create a strong harmony, look for a particular temperature of color, warm or cool. Some perceive this combination as less vibrant than complimentary, but the use of three colors from the wheel can give a dramatic effect.

It is more impactful to use three colors on a twelve-color wheel, all next to each other. Examples would be green, yellow-green and yellow or red, red-violet and violet. To create the best effect, one color should be dominant. This combination creates a sense of variety, and a good effect.

Picture 15 Split-Complimentary

*Split-Complementary Scheme*

<u>A main color and two colors on each side of its complimentary on the opposite side on the wheel.</u>

Split-complementary color scheme has the same strong visual contrast as the complementary color but may have more harmony but use your head. Some colors should not be mixed. For example, the main color of yellow can mix with the two additional colors of red/purple and blue/purple for a nice contrast. Usually, yellows and greens plus reds and purples are good. This scheme can avoid fatigue and maintain a high contrast.

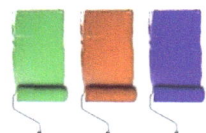Picture 16 Triad

*Triad Scheme*

<u>Three colors evenly spaced around the wheel.</u>

This scheme retains harmony and high contrast even when pale hues are used. Use a triangle of equal sides on the wheel to find the triadic colors. Popular among artists, this scheme offers a strong visual and richness.

An example would be red, blue and yellow. This combination creates contrast while retaining balance, richness, and harmony. It is pleasing to the eye.

 Picture 17 warm and cool

 Picture 18 warm

*Warm*
Range from red to yellow.
These colors do exactly what they are called: create warmth, happiness, and heat. You might think of the sun, fire or perhaps the passion of love. The color of red-violet is right between a warm and cool color so is neither or both in attributes. Warm colors energize. Take a look at orange.

 Picture 19 cool

*Cool*
Range from green to purple.
These colors might emulate winter, night, nature and water. Yellow-green is right between cool and warm so is considered neither or both in attributes. Cool colors are relaxing, calm and trustful. Take a look at purple that exemplifies royal and elegant.

 Picture 20 neutral

*Neutral*
Not usually found on the color wheel.

Most neutral colors fall under the definition of white, black, tan, gold, ivory, silver, brown, cream, beige, or gray. The theory of neutral colors help put the focus on other colors or to tone down some intense ones and become the backdrop to design. This usually means without color, but most of the neutrals appear to have undertones of color. For example, beige might take an undertone of pink or gold, or white might be slightly blue. Be aware of these underlying tones as you match or choose paint. Some neutrals are warm such as beige or brown while others are cold such as white or silver. Although these attributes exist, they are far more subtle than the hues of yellow or orange.

*Tints, Shades, and Tone*

Picture 21 Tint

*Tints*

Add white.

It is frequently referred to as a shimmer; the resulting color is lighter than the original.

A tint can be called a pastel, add white to a color and there you have it. You can even combine colors on the wheel and add white to create a unique tint. Lighting can range from extremely pale to a barely tinted pure color. When tinting think of soothing, youthful and feminine attributes. Think of light green as a tint of green.

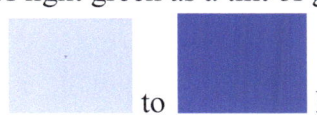Picture 22 Shade, light to dark

*Shade*

Add black.

When you add black, the color can go from a barely shaded hue to extremely dark. Black can quickly destroy the main color, so use wisely, it can become overpowering.

When shading, think powerful, mysterious and masculine attributes. An example of a shade would be dark green versus light green. You may ask, where is brown? Brown is just a shade of reddish-orange.

 Picture 23 Tone

*Tone*

Add any grayscale color.

To tone down a color is to make it more appealing and softer.

Tones, for some reason, are more pleasing to the eye. Any color where gray has been added is said to be toned down.

You can tint, shade or tone down any of the hues on the color wheel. You can also accent your color scheme by adding touches of one or more colors. Be aware that tints, tones and shades change the emotional meanings. They tend to slant the reactions to the softer side, when using white, or the stronger side, with black. Shades or tints may have different meanings. Colors change when lightened, darkened, combined with other colors or shaded.

*Embedding*

Color within another.

A color within another color can create a new context around an image. Even the same color can look different on different backgrounds.

How do these colors look to you? Yellow on black looks brilliant while washed out on the white background. Yellow on red might suggest passion and a fun place to go. Fast-food restaurants might use this combination as it prompts people to move in and out quickly, energized.

## Other Words to Know

Terms we will not discuss in this Series, but brief descriptions follow. This is not an all-inclusive listing but takes some of the common phrases and defines them for the reader.

*Lightness*
The quality or condition of being illuminated. In color, it is the calculation of how much the object appears to reflect or transmit light.

*Brightness*
Intensity of color, not a property

*Achromatic:*
Free of color or colorless

*Balance*
Achieving color or harmony

*Carried Color*
Colors in an image laid on a background

*Chromaticity or Chroma*
Having pure color, no addition of gray, white or black. The colors appear vivid.

*Color Palette*
A planned arrangement of colors meant to be viewed as a whole

*Color Scheme*
Describes a group of colors to be used in art and design

*Color Temperature*
Refers to the warmth or coolness of a color

*Intensity*
Brightness of a colors purity or saturation. Intensity refers to the purity of a hue. Intensity is also known as saturation for painters. For physicists, intensity refers to radiation. The highest intensity or purity of a hue is the hue as it appears in the spectrum or on the color wheel.

*Pure*
Maximum saturation, not mixed with other colors
*Saturation*
Saturation defines a range of color from pure (100%) to gray (0%). A pure color is fully saturated. Desaturated colors are considered dull and lifeless but can also be perceived as softer while saturated colors are perceived as vivid and bright but can also be shocking. It can also be called a color's intensity.
*Value*
Color also has value, a relative degree of lightness or darkness. Most colors are recognizable in a full range of values; we identify as a form of "red" everything from the palest pink to the darkest maroon. Value is a measure of the brightness of a color.

You will now enter the world of color, what each one means to you and when to use it. Each primary, secondary, tertiary, and neutral color is discussed as they apply to business applications. Look to Book 2 to get color definitions and Book 3 for a how-to guide for picking the perfect colors that represent you and your brand. Book 2 also talks about meanings related to the specific color, international meanings, a listing of example services and businesses that might use the color and examples of combinations. A generic color definition is also added. These usually comprise all meanings throughout time so have limited uses and testing for authenticity. Some words, such as calming, energetic and peaceful are over used and do not necessarily represent experiment results from today. Search for brands on the internet that use the colors you are looking at and see what type of company it is. Keep a journal and record all of your findings from here on out, if you have not started already.

## **Chapter 8 Summary**

The first in the Series, 'Color Me Successful, How Color Sells Your Brand: Book 1 Color Theory', lays out the foundation for the small business owner to understand how color started, developed and is used today for several applications. By understanding the reasons for color reaction, you can successfully use it to enhance your brands, logos, advertising and marketing. It will help drive people to your business, product or service by re-enforcing feelings and make them buy from you. It is critical in product design and signage. Color has the power to change the physiology and mental states to alter the way our brain relates to the outside world.

As you learned, color started with art and print as a pigment. The original theory revolved around three primary colors: red, blue and yellow (RYB model). It took to 1665 when Isaac Newton experimented with the prism, to realize that color also was a spectrum of light each onehaving a distinction wavelength. This leads us to the conclusion that color in painting, pigment and printing is different than color on computer screens and phones (electronics). As the science evolved, the scheme for printing went from RYB to CYMK and for electronics to RGB.

As stated above, let's look at color as energy and understand how you and your brain receive this information and therefore, react to it. Colors are spectrums of light that are seen through your pupil and processed by cone and rod receptors at the back of your retina. A simple representation, if you would like more information, please go to the appendix at the back of this or read Chapter 4 over. The key out of this chapter is; your brain is the driving force to how you and your customers relate to color. The reactions affect what you see, combined with cultural, learned and behavioral traits, as well.

The human eye can see 1 to 10 million colors depending on whose study you quote. To use color effectively, you must create a pleasing arrangement, simply put, something that someone wants to look at. With this many options you can see, and combinations, you need to understand color harmony, how they look together to produce a simple, soothing effect to the viewer. Color harmony is all about understanding the wheel and how to have colors interact successfully with each other.

The traditional wheel was based upon the primary colors of red, yellow and blue, which I will use, to keep it simple. Further in this Series discusses color as it pertains to electronics, such as websites, as well as the expanded CYMK model for printing. The traditional wheel has 12 colors on it: 3 primary, 3 secondary and 6 tertiary. By mixing, tinting, shading and many other things, colors can be created but must be functionally appealing while sensitive to cultural and behavioral traits. The key here is, color must capture your client quickly and help them remember your message through connection and emotion. The different schemes that work successfully for color choices are monochromatic, complimentary, analogous, split-complimentary and triad.

Let us not forget warm and cool. Warm colors create happiness that can energize, such as our sun. Cool colors provide a feeling of calm and trust; examples might be water and nature.

There are many other ways to manipulate color through tints, shades, and tones. Colors can be manipulated but after reading this and doing the assignment, you will be on your way to understanding how to pick and learn why certain colors for your brand, marketing material, and website work.

Book 2 - Color Emotions, will look at each primary, secondary and tertiary color and define how to use them together. See you in the next one of the Series.

## Appendix - References

1. How Do Colors Affect Purchases?, Kissmetrics, https://blog.kissmetrics.com/color-psychology/

2. Do you see what I see?, 2011, BBC News Science and Environment, http://www.bbc.co.uk/news/science-environment-14421303

3. Cooper, Kim and Kazilek, CJ, Seeing Color , ASU School of Life Sciences, by Kim Cooper and CJ Kazilek https://askabiologist.asu.edu/explore/seeing-color

4. Oracle Think Quest, Colors

5. Empower Yourself With Color Psychology, Color Psychology to Empower and Inspire You, http://www.empower-yourself-with-color-psychology.com/

6. Snell, Steven, Colors in corporate branding design, 2009, Smashing Magazine , http://www.smashingmagazine.com/2009/01/colors-in-corporate-branding-and-design/

7. Stanger, Melissa, How Brands Use The Psychology Of Color To Manipulate You , 2012, Business Insider, http://www.businessinsider.com/branding-and-the-psychology-of-color-2012-12

8. Eric Markowitz ,| How to Choose the Right Colors for Your Brand , 2010, INC. http://www.inc.com/guides/2010/10/how-to-choose-the-right-colors-for-your-brand.html

9. Miller, Jason True Colors: What Your Brand Colors Say About Your Business [Infographic] June 26, 2012, Marketo Blog, http://blog.marketo.com/2012/06/true-colors-what-your-brand-colors-say-about-your-business.html

10. How We See Color?, Pantone, http://www.pantone.com/pages/pantone/Pantone.aspx?pg=19357&ca=29

11. Patrick, Brian, <u>5 Secrets for Making Your Logo Stand Out</u>, June 14, 2013, Entrepreneur, http://www.entrepreneur.com/article/227017

12. <u>The Meaning of Colours</u>, Sibagraphics, <u>The Meaning of Colours</u>, Sibagraphics

13. Lidwell, William, Professor .<u>How Colors Affect You: What Science Reveals</u>, The Great Courses, http://www.thegreatcourses.com/courses/how-colors-affect-you-what-science-reveals.html

14. Chapman, Cameron, Color Theory for Designers Part 1, The Meaning of Color, May 28, 2010, http://www.smashingmagazine.com/2010/01/color-theory-for-designers-part-1-the-meaning-of-color/

15. Chapman, Cameron, Color Theory for Designers Part 2, Understanding Concepts and Terminology, Feb. 2, 2010 http://www.smashingmagazine.com/2010/02/color-theory-for-designers-part-2-understanding-concepts-and-terminology/

16. Chapman, Camerson, Color Theory for Designer Part 3, Creating Your Own color Palettes, Feb. 9, 2010, http://www.smashingmagazine.com/2010/02/color-theory-for-designer-part-3-creating-your-own-color-palettes/

17. Empower Yourself with Color Psychology, http://www.empower-yourself-with-color-psychology.com/cultural-color.html

18. De Bortoli, Mario, Maroto, Jesus, Translating Colours, http://globalpropaganda.com/articles/TranslatingColours.pdf

19. Colour Blindness Experience it, http://www.colourblindawareness.org/colour-blindness/colour-blindness-experience-it/

20. Color Blindness Topic Overview, http://www.webmd.com/eye-health/tc/color-blindness-topic-overview

21. Wade, Nicolas, With Genetic Gift Two Monkeys are Viewing a More Colorful World, Sept. 21, 2009, NY Times, http://www.nytimes.com/2009/09/22/science/22gene.html?_r=0

22. Color and Its Influence, http://www.greatestlook.com/advice/color_influence.htm

23. What Is Colorblindness and the Different Types, http://colorvisiontesting.com/color2.htm

24. Color, 2013 http://www.cs.stedwards.edu/~tmclero/cosc4351/project1/project1.html

25. Lidz, Gogo, a cure for color blindness that isn't just monky business, May 10, 2015, Newsweek, http://www.newsweek.com/cure-color-blindness-isnt-just-monkey-business-330258

26. Yam, Kimberly, New glasses Transform The Way Colorblind People See The World, Jan. 13, 2015, Huffington Post, http://www.huffingtonpost.com/2015/01/13/color-blindness-correcting-glasses_n_6446094.html

27. The 28 best tools for choosing a colour scheme, Oct. 24, 2014, http://www.creativebloq.com/colour/tools-colour-schemes-12121430

28. Color Terminology, http://www.colorbasics.com/Glossary/

29. Basci color schemes - Introduction to Color Theory, http://www.tigercolor.com/color-lab/color-theory/color-theory-intro.htm

30. Color Harmonies, http://www.tigercolor.com/color-lab/color-theory/color-harmonies.htm

31. Porter, Jane, 5 Ways Store Colors Can Influence Shoppers, July 24, 2012, Entrepreneur, http://www.entrepreneur.com/article/223799

32. Ciotti, Gregory, The Psychology of Color in Marketing and Branding, May 15, 2014, Entrepreneur, http://www.entrepreneur.com/article/233843

# **Extra Section: Color Blindness, what do you see**

Colorblindness affects approximately 5-8% of men and 0.5% of women. Why more men are colorblind than women? If genetic, inherited, the most common form, it is related to the X chromosome and, therefore, more common in males. Of these people, 99% are red and green weak. Another type is blue-green colorblindness followed by a rare condition of, complete absence of color vision or total colorblindness. Its effects can be mild to severe, as well, meaning the ability to see certain colors is from slight to strong. Colorblindness does not mean an individual is blind, but they have a deficiency or inability to see a color under normal lighting conditions. It can be genetic, caused by physical or chemical damage to the eye or damage to the brain. It can also result with age mostly because of cataracts. This can be problematic because any color that contains red or green can have a different effect. For example, purple, which contains red, would look like blue. Although not life threatening, colorblindness can affect something as simple as choosing clothes to wear. Try http://wwwvischeck.com to upload photos and files and then convert them to colorblind vision.

I have mentioned throughout that colors are different wavelengths of visible light and mixtures of different wavelengths produce different colors. People can feel the energy deposited by the light and, therefore, are convinced that the light exists but to a visually impaired person, there is no connection between the specific energy and a color. To connect the color to the energy, it must be a taught response.

There is hope, though. New glasses can transform the way colorblind people see the world allowing them to see hues they may not have ever seen before. Also, a landmark experiment of injecting a viral vector behind the retinas of a colorblind breed of monkey allowed the monkey to see color. Why would a colorblind person do any of this? The answer is simple; we live in a world full of color. Tasks such as driving, cooking, sports, and nature are all enhanced with color. In business, it is a detriment not to see color. Much information can be lost to people with even a mild form of blindness. What is red and what is orange on a pie chart, for example.

How does this affect using color on your website, brand, and marketing? It depends on who your client is. I mentioned above that 5-8% of men are colorblind, mostly the most common form, green/red. That means that approximately 10.5 million men are colorblind. Your assignment in 1 was to define your client exactly, so pull out your description. Are most of your customers men? Also, seniors tend to become visually impaired as they age. Does it make sense for you to address color blindness in seniors when designing your website, brand, and marketing material? You can address some things immediately. Instead of using a green or red button for your give away or call-to-action, use yellow or blue. Make sure that all things have enough verbiage for explanations or do things such as underline links. If you can't see the colors, underline means a link. Packaging not only should have color but also written product information, I bet you have never considered any of this, and you may not need to. It all depends on your client base, and how important it is to get to this group of people.

## **Assignment**

I want you to have a blank journal for this journey. You will be evaluating many things, and you need a place to write them down and record them. You will go back to this journal many times throughout this Series to re-read and ponder your decisions.

In addition, I want you to start searching for the websites of your competitors. Look at the colors used, write down what you like and don't about the look, service description, and flow. Spend some time on the brand. What colors does your industry commonly use? How does it make you feel and how does it flow? Write this all down in your journal.

## About the author:

Judy Haar has been a mentor for hundreds of businesses through SCORE, America's Counselors to Small Business. She has advised owners on website design, marketing, branding, business plans, and social media, to name a few. She is a marketing expert and was a senior executive in a firm that did branding, merchandising, design/build, and architecture for financial institutions. Judy has continued her expertise through university courses and real life examples in the area of website design, social media and advertising.

Discover other titles by Author name on Amazon
For I Am With You
Death Tones: Short Stories About Transformation
Color Me Successful Book 2 Color Theory
Color Me Successful Book 3 Color Marketing
Follow the Light- Write Your Journey

Connect with Me Online
http://www.emergencepublishinggroup.com
http://www.facBook.com/judyhaarauthor

Please leave a review for this Book. Thank you.

www.ingramcontent.com/pod-product-compliance
Lightning Source LLC
Chambersburg PA
CBHW040330220526
45473CB00009B/2635